BLAZERS™

MONSTERS

Zombies

by Mari C. Schuh and Aaron Sautter

Reading Consultant:
Barbara J. Fox
Reading Specialist
North Carolina State University

Content Consultant:
David D. Gilmore
Professor of Anthropology
Stony Brook University
Stony Brook, New York

Capstone
press®

Mankato, Minnesota

Blazers is published by Capstone Press,
151 Good Counsel Drive, P.O. Box 669, Mankato, Minnesota 56002.
www.capstonepress.com

Library of Congress Cataloging-in-Publication Data
Schuh, Mari C., 1975–
    Zombies / Mari C. Schuh, Aaron Sautter.
    p. cm.—(Blazers. Monsters)
    Summary: "A brief explanation of the legendary monsters called
zombies, including their development through history and their use in
popular culture"—Provided by publisher.
    Includes bibliographical references and index.
    ISBN-13: 978-0-7368-6446-6 (hardcover)
    ISBN-10: 0-7368-6446-6 (hardcover)
    1. Zombies—Juvenile literature. I. Sautter, Aaron. II. Title. III. Series.
GR581.S34 2007
398'.45—dc22   2006000497

Editorial Credits
Jennifer Besel, editor; Juliette Peters, designer; Kelly Garvin,
    photo researcher/photo editor

Photo Credits
Capstone Press/Karon Dubke, cover, 4–5, 6, 7, 8–9, 26–27
Corbis/Bettman, 14–15; John Springer Collection, 12; Michael
    Gibson/Universal Studios/Zuma, 22, 22–23
Fortean Picture Library/Virgil Finlay, 11
Getty Images Inc./Amanda Edwards, 25; Kevin Winter, 28–29; Pictorial
    Parade/Hulton Archive, 16–17
SuperStock/age fotostock, 18–19
Zuma Press/Universal Pictures, 24; Working Title Films, 20–21

**Co-author Mari C. Schuh dedicates this book to her brothers Ryan and John,
longtime fans of Rob Zombie.**

Table of Contents

A Dark Walk Home

A woman strolls home after a night at the movies. Shivering in the cold, she takes a shortcut through the graveyard.

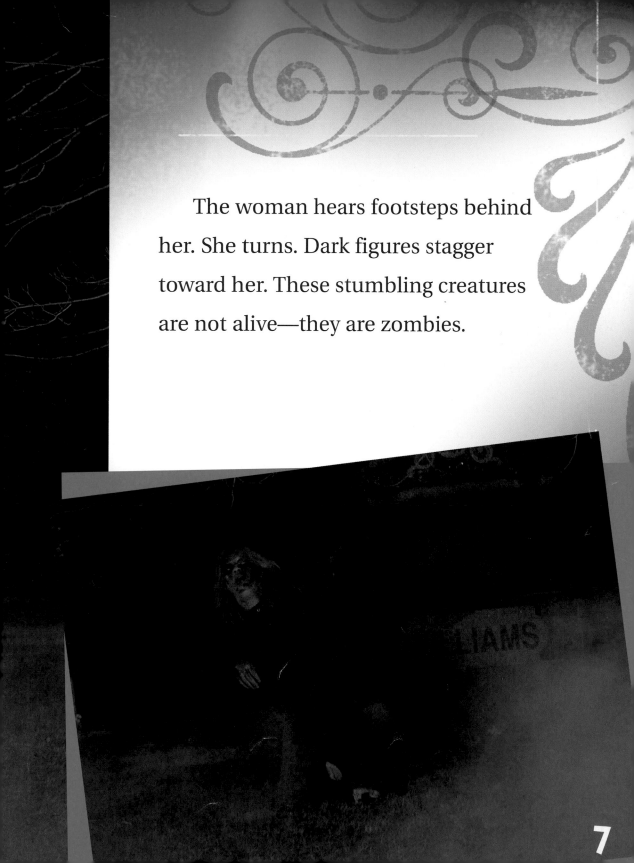

The woman hears footsteps behind her. She turns. Dark figures stagger toward her. These stumbling creatures are not alive—they are zombies.

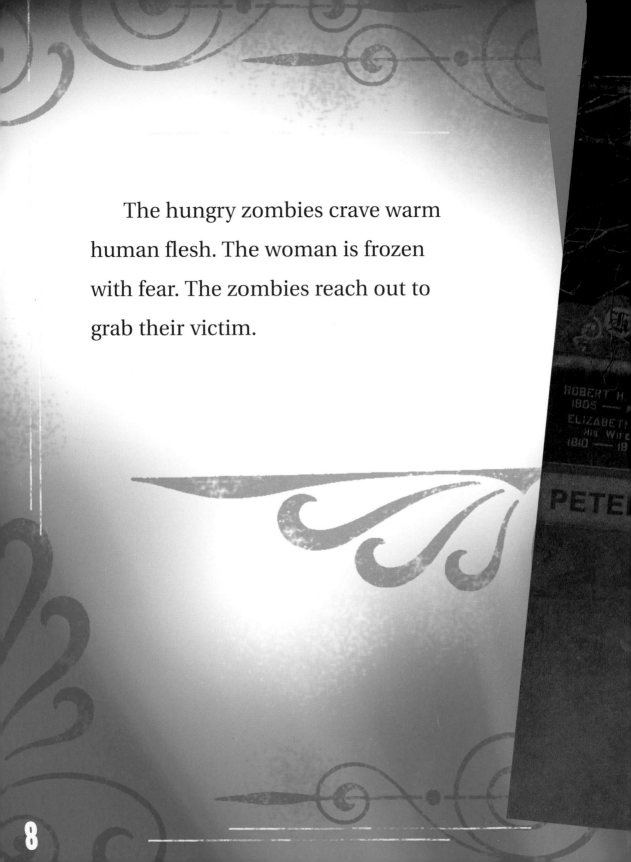

The hungry zombies crave warm human flesh. The woman is frozen with fear. The zombies reach out to grab their victim.

Made-up Monsters

For more than a hundred years, people have been frightened by zombie legends. But these creepy creatures don't really exist. Zombies are simply made-up monsters.

Zombie legends began in the country of Haiti. These stories soon spread around the world. In the 1930s, moviemakers joined in on the fun and made films about these scary monsters.

By the 1970s, movie zombies had become the smelly, rotting monsters we know today. These zombies stumble around hunting for people to eat.

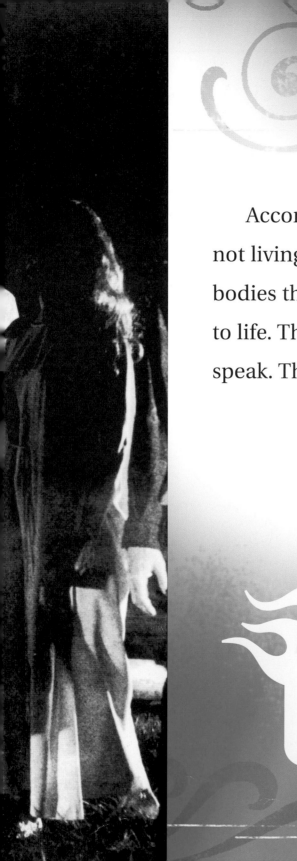

According to legend, zombies are not living people. Zombies are dead bodies that have been brought back to life. These monsters can't think or speak. They only groan and eat.

BLAZER FACT

In movies, zombies do not sleep. In fact, they never even need to rest.

18

Movies use many ways to explain how zombies come to life. Objects from space, chemicals, and nasty diseases have all been blamed for creating zombies.

BLAZER FACT

In the movies, being bitten by a zombie is another sure way to become one.

With unblinking eyes, zombies stagger across movie screens toward the living. They want warm, soft flesh. They crave plump, tasty brains.

BLAZER FACT

Movie zombies are always hungry. No matter how much a zombie eats, there is still room for another bite.

In films, zombies always chase after people, even after losing their arms or legs.

Zombies are already dead, so they do not feel pain. In most movies, the only way to kill a zombie is to destroy its brain.

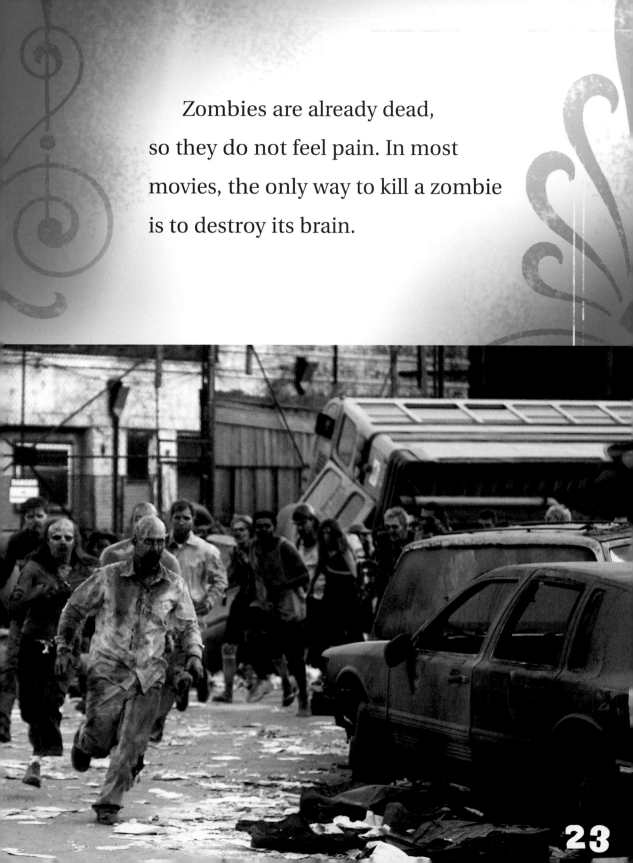

Finding Zombies Today

Zombies aren't just popular in movies. You can read about them in books. There are lots of stories about zombies on the Internet as well.

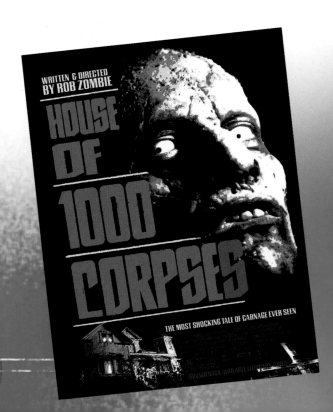

WRITTEN & DIRECTED BY ROB ZOMBIE

HOUSE OF 1000 CORPSES

THE MOST SHOCKING TALE OF CARNAGE EVER SEEN

Zombies are also fun monsters in video games. Some games let you be the hero who kills the zombies. In other games, you can even be the zombie.

BLAZER FACT

Some zombie video games are so popular that they have been made into movies.

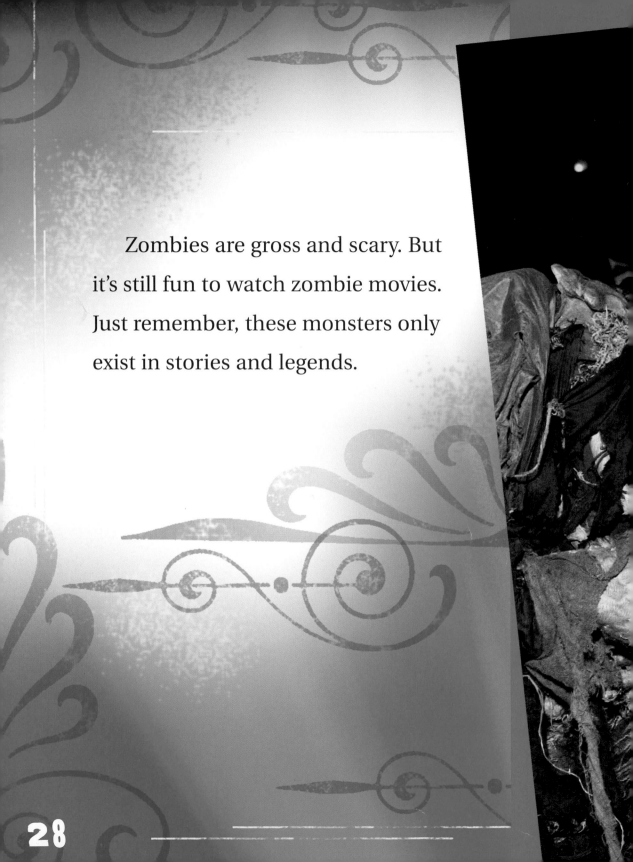

Zombies are gross and scary. But it's still fun to watch zombie movies. Just remember, these monsters only exist in stories and legends.

Glossary

chemical (KEM-uh-kuhl)—a substance that creates a reaction

crave (KRAVE)—to want something very much

exist (eg-ZIST)—to live or to be real

flesh (FLESH)—the soft part of a person's or animal's body that covers the bones

graveyard (GRAYV-yard)—a piece of land where dead people are buried

stagger (STAG-ur)—to walk unsteadily

victim (VIK-tuhm)—a person who is hurt, killed, or made to suffer

MONSTERS

Read More

Forget, Thomas. *Introducing Zombies.* Famous Movie Monsters. New York: Rosen, 2006.

Herbst, Judith. *Monsters.* The Unexplained. Minneapolis: Lerner, 2005.

Internet Sites

FactHound offers a safe, fun way to find Internet sites related to this book. All of the sites on FactHound have been researched by our staff.

Here's how:

1. Visit *www.facthound.com*

2. Choose your grade level.

3. Type in this book ID **0736864466** for age-appropriate sites. You may also browse subjects by clicking on letters, or by clicking on pictures and words.

4. Click on the **Fetch It** button.

FactHound will fetch the best sites for you!

Index